AAT

AAT Basic Accounting I

Pocket notes

KAPLAN

PUBLISHING

British library cataloguing-in-publication data

A catalogue record for this book is available from the British Library.

Published by:
Kaplan Publishing UK
Unit 2 The Business Centre
Molly Millars Lane
Wokingham
Berkshire
RG41 2QZ

ISBN 978-0-85732-636-2

© Kaplan Financial Limited, 2012

Printed and bound in Great Britain.

CONTENTS

Preface

These pocket notes contain the key things that you need to know for the exam, presented in a unique visual way that makes revision easy and effective.

Written by experienced lecturers and authors, these pocket notes break down content into manageable chunks to maximise your concentration.

A guide to the assessment

- The assessment.
- Terminology.

The assessment

Basic Accounting I (BAI) is the first of two financial accounting assessments at level 2. It should be studied and taken before Basic Accounting II (BAII).

Examination

Basic Accounting I (BAI) is assessed by means of a computer based assessment.

The exam will be for a duration of two hours and will be assessed by computer.

You will be required to demonstrate competence in both sections of the assessment.

The BAI assessment consists of sixteen tasks, six in Section 1 and ten in Section 2.

The examination will typically involve the following:

- making entries in the sales, purchases and returns day books, and transferring the totals to the sales, purchases and general ledger
- making entries in the cash book and the petty cash book, and to transfer the totals to the sales, purchases and general ledger
- dealing with documents that are sent to and from organisations
- coding and filing those documents appropriately.

Terminology

From January 2012, all AAT assessments have fully adopted international accounting standards.

The table below provides a summary of the UK terms and the International terms that are now in use. The summary does not provide a comprehensive list, it just details the terms you are likely to find in the BAI and BAII assessments. .

UK	International
Fixed assets	Non-current assets
Stock	Inventory
Debtor (SLCA)	Receivable (SLCA)
Creditor (PLCA)	Payable (PLCA)

As you progress onto the next level of the qualification you will need to become aware of more international terminology.

It is also important for you to be aware that the terms "main ledger" and "general ledger" are interchangeable in practice. The AAT assessments will refer to "general ledger". Please don't let the different use of terms cause confusion.

1

Double entry bookkeeping

- Principles of double entry bookkeeping.
- The accounting equation.

Principles of double entry bookkeeping

Principles

Dual effect
- each transaction has two financial effects

Separate entity
- the owner of the business is a separate entity from the business.

Therefore:

- each transaction has both a debit and a credit entry in the ledger accounts.

- the amount invested into the business by the owner is kept separate, it is known as "capital" as is the amount withdrawn from the business by the owner for their own personal use, it is known as "drawings".
- Note: capital and drawings are not necessarily just cash, an owner can invest and withdraw other assets such as inventory or even non-current assets. amount taken out by the owner = drawings.

Accounting equation

Assets – Liabilities = Capital

Terminology

Asset
- something owned by the business

Liability
- something owed by the business

Capital
- amount the owner has invested in the business

Receivable
- someone who owes the business money

Payable
- someone the business owes money to

Chapter 1

The accounting equation

Example

Accounting equation

(i) Ted pays £10,000 into a business bank account to start a business.

Dual effect	Assets (cash)		Capital
	£10,000	=	£10,000

(ii) Ted buys goods to resell for £3,000 in cash

Dual effect	Assets (cash) + assets (inventory)		Capital
	£7,000 + £3,000	=	£10,000

(iii) Ted sells the goods for cash for £4,000.

These goods were bought for £3,000, which is £1,000 less than what they have now been sold for. Therefore, a profit of £1,000 has been made.

This is added to the capital balance as it is an increase in the amount owed back to the owner of the business.

Dual effect	Assets (cash)		Capital		Profit
	£11,000	=	£10,000	+	£1,000

(iv) Ted purchases more goods for £6,000 on credit

Dual effect	Assets (inventory)	Liabilities (payable)		Capital + Profit
	£11,000 + £6,000	− £6,000	=	£11,000

(v) Ted sells these goods for £8,000 on credit

Dual effect	Assets (receivables) − Liabilities		Capital + Profit
	£11,000 + £8,000 − £6,000	=	£11,000 + £2,000

(vi) Ted pays £500 of rent for his premises. This reduces his cash and profit by £500

Dual effect

Assets (cash)		Capital + Profit
£10,500 + £8,000 − £6,000	=	£11,000 + £1,500

2

Ledger accounting

- Ledger accounts.
- General rules of double entry bookkeeping.
- Accounting for cash transactions.
- Accounting for credit transactions.

Ledger accounts

Typical ledger account:

Title of account

Date Narrative	£	Date Narrative	£
DEBIT side		CREDIT side	

The dual effect means that every transaction has a debit entry in one account and a credit entry in another account.

Key question – which account is the debit entry to and which account is the credit entry to?

Definition

A **cash transaction** means a transaction which is paid for immediately.

Definition

A **credit transaction** is a transaction that is only paid after an agreed period of time, e.g. 30 days.

Note that the terms 'cash', 'cheque' are used interchangeably in the early part of your studies. If the person pays by cash or cheque, the money will be entered into the 'bank' account (sometimes called the 'cash account').

Thus if John buys a car for £4,000 and pays immediately with a cheque or cash, that is a cash transaction.

If John buys a car for £4,000 on credit, when he eventually pays he can pay with either cash or a cheque – it makes no difference – it will be a credit transaction.

General rules of double entry bookkeeping

The table below summarises the effect a debit (DR) or a credit (CR) entry can have.

Ledger account

DEBIT £	CREDIT £
Money in	Money out
Increase in asset	Increase in liability
Decrease in liability	Decrease in asset
Expense	Income

The mnemonic **DEAD CLIC** is a great way to remember the side to post a debit or credit entry to.

DRs increase;	CRs increase;
Expenses	**L**iabilities
Assets	**I**ncome
Drawings	**C**apital

Accounting for cash transactions

Cash transactions

(i) Payment of £10,000 into business bank account by owner:

Debit Bank (money in)

Credit Capital (increase in liability – amount owed to owner)

Bank account			
	£		£
Capital	10,000		

Capital account			
	£		£
		Bank	10,000

(ii) Purchase of goods for cash of £3,000

Debit Purchases (expense)

Credit Bank (money out)

Purchases account			
	£		£
Bank	10,000		

Bank account			
	£		£
		Purchases	3,000

(iii) Sale of goods for cash of £4,000
  Debit Bank (money in)
  Credit Sales (income)

Bank account		
	£	£
Sales	4,000	

Sales account		
	£	£
		Bank	4,000

(iv) Payment of rent in cash £500
  Debit Rent (expense)
  Credit Bank (money out)

Rent account		
	£	£
Bank	500	

Bank account		
	£	£
		Rent	500

Accounting for credit transactions

(i) Purchases goods for £6,000 on credit
   Debit   Purchases (expense)
   Credit Payables (liability)

Purchases account			
	£		£
Payables	6,000		

Payables account			
	£		£
		Purchases	6,000

(ii) Sale of goods on credit for £8,000
   Debit   Receivables (asset)
   Credit Sales (income)

Receivables account			
	£		£
Sales	8,000		

Sales account			
	£		£
		Receivables	8,000

(iii) Payment of part of money owed to credit supplier of £1,500

Debit   Payables (reduction in liability)
Credit Bank (money out)

Payables account		
	£	£
Bank	1,500	

Bank account		
	£	£
	Payables	1,500

(iv) Receipt of part of money owed by credit customer of £5,000

Debit   Bank (money in)
Credit Receivables (reduction in asset)

Bank account		
	£	£
Receivables	5,000	

Receivables account		
	£	£
	Bank	5,000

3

Drafting an initial trial balance

- Balancing the ledger accounts.
- What is a trial balance?

Balancing the ledger accounts

At various points in time the owner/owners of a business will need information about the total transactions in the period. E.g. total sales, amount of payables outstanding, amount of cash remaining. This can be found by balancing the ledger accounts.

Example

Here is a typical cash (or bank) account:

Cash account

	£		£
Capital	10,000	Purchases	3,000
Sales	4,000	Rent	500
Receivables	5,000	Payables	1,500

Step 1 Total both the debit side and the credit side and make a note of the totals.

Step 2 The higher of the totals should be inserted at the bottom of both the debit side and the credit side (leaving a line before inserting the totals).

Cash account

	£		£
Capital	10,000	Purchases	3,000
Sales	4,000	Rent	500
Receivables	5,000	Payables	1,500
	19,000		19,000

Step 3 On the side that amounts to the lowest total, insert the figure that makes that side add up to the higher total. This balance should have the narrative "balance carried down" ("balance c/d").

Cash account

	£		£
Capital	10,000	Purchases	3,000
Sales	4,000	Rent	500
Receivables	5,000	Payables	1,500
		Balance c/d	14,000
	19,000		19,000

Step 4 On the opposite side to where the "balance carried down" has been inserted, enter the same figure below the total line. This should be referred to as "balance brought down" ("balance b/d").

Cash account

	£		£
Capital	10,000	Purchases	3,000
Sales	4,000	Rent	500
Receivables	5,000	Payables	1,500
		Balance c/d	14,000
	19,000		19,000
Balance b/d	14,000		

This shows that after all of these transactions there is £14,000 of cash left as an asset in the business (a debit balance brought down = an asset).

CBA focus

In the examination you will be required to balance a number of ledger accounts and you must be able to select the correct narratives to be used when balancing an account off.

What is a trial balance?

- list of all of the ledger balances in the general ledger
- debit balances and credit balances listed separately
- debit balance total should equal credit balance total.

Example

Trial balance

	Debit balances £	Credit balances £
Sales		5,000
Wages	100	
Purchases	3,000	
Rent	200	
Car	3,000	
Receivables	100	
Payables		1,400
	6,400	6,400

Debit or credit balance?

If you are just given a list of balances you must know whether they are debit or credit balances.

Remember the rules!

CBA focus

In the examination you will either have to enter a number of balances in the trial balance from ledger accounts that have been balanced or you will be given a list of balances that you then have to determine which side of the trial balance they should appear on.

Debit balances	Credit balances
Asset	Liability
Expense	Income
Drawings	Capital

4

Credit sales: documents

- Sales on credit – documents.
- Preparing a sales invoice.

Sales on credit – documents

Documents issued during the making of sales on credit:

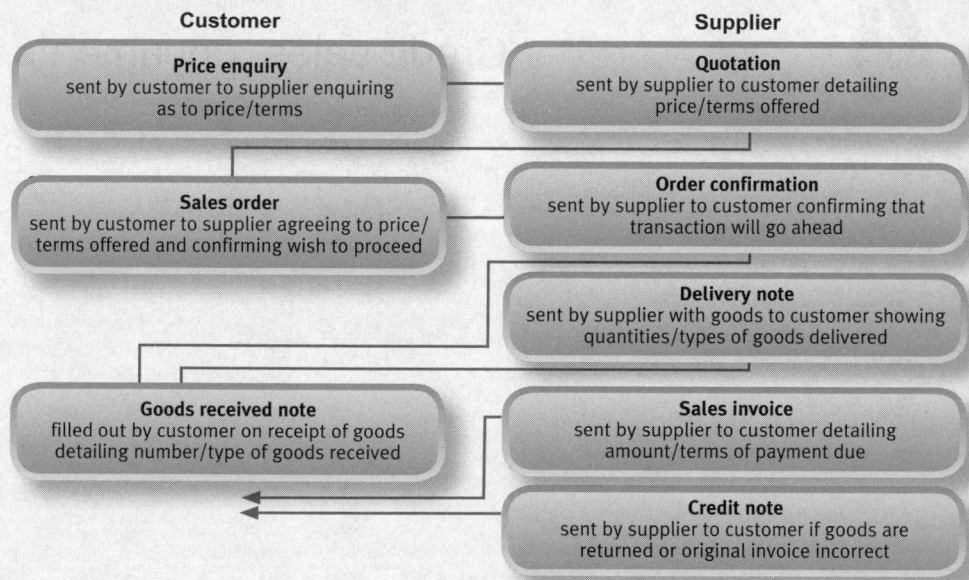

Customer | **Supplier**

Price enquiry
sent by customer to supplier enquiring as to price/terms

Quotation
sent by supplier to customer detailing price/terms offered

Sales order
sent by customer to supplier agreeing to price/terms offered and confirming wish to proceed

Order confirmation
sent by supplier to customer confirming that transaction will go ahead

Delivery note
sent by supplier with goods to customer showing quantities/types of goods delivered

Goods received note
filled out by customer on receipt of goods detailing number/type of goods received

Sales invoice
sent by supplier to customer detailing amount/terms of payment due

Credit note
sent by supplier to customer if goods are returned or original invoice incorrect

Chapter 4

Preparing a sales invoice

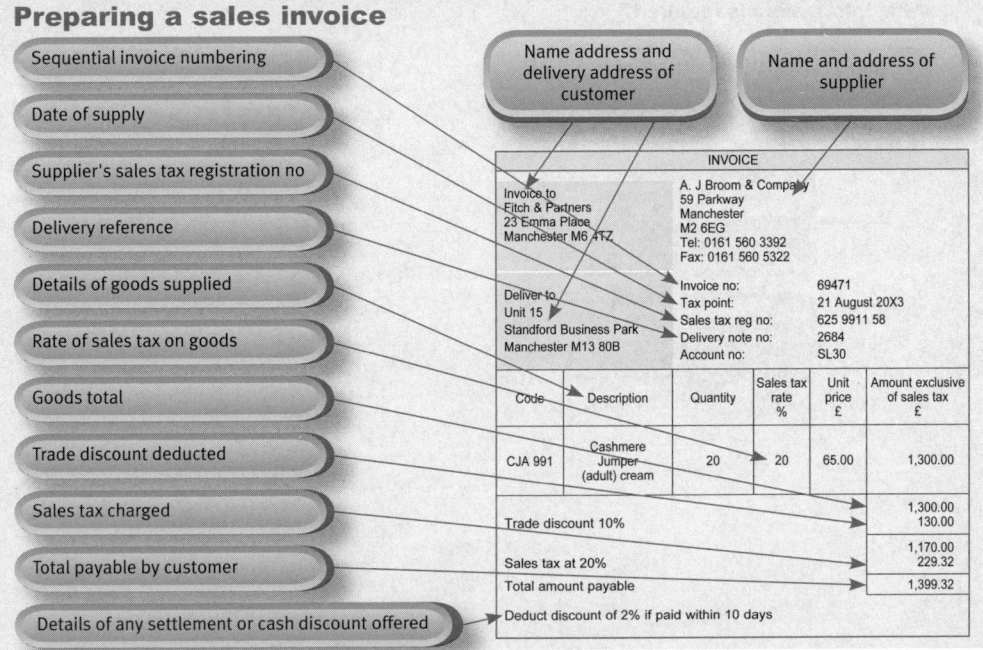

Sequential invoice numbering

Date of supply

Supplier's sales tax registration no

Delivery reference

Details of goods supplied

Rate of sales tax on goods

Goods total

Trade discount deducted

Sales tax charged

Total payable by customer

Details of any settlement or cash discount offered

Name address and delivery address of customer

Name and address of supplier

INVOICE

Invoice to
Fitch & Partners
23 Emma Place
Manchester M6 4TZ

A. J Broom & Company
59 Parkway
Manchester
M2 6EG
Tel: 0161 560 3392
Fax: 0161 560 5322

Deliver to
Unit 15
Standford Business Park
Manchester M13 80B

Invoice no:	69471				
Tax point:	21 August 20X3				
Sales tax reg no:	625 9911 58				
Delivery note no:	2684				
Account no:	SL30				

Code	Description	Quantity	Sales tax rate %	Unit price £	Amount exclusive of sales tax £
CJA 991	Cashmere Jumper (adult) cream	20	20	65.00	1,300.00

	1,300.00
Trade discount 10%	130.00
	1,170.00
Sales tax at 20%	229.32
Total amount payable	1,399.32

Deduct discount of 2% if paid within 10 days

What information is required?

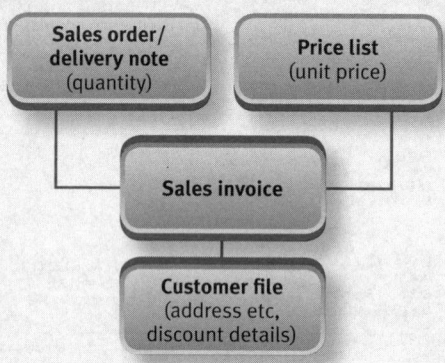

5

Credit sales: sales tax and discounts

- Types of discounts.
- Sales tax and settlement discounts.
- Preparing credit notes.
- Coding.

Types of discounts

Trade discount
% **deducted** from list price for certain valued customers – shown on face of invoice.

Bulk discount
% **deducted** from list price for certain quantity purchased – shown on face of invoice.

Settlement discount
% **offered** to certain customers for payment within a certain time period – shown at bottom of invoice

CBA focus

The examination requires you to be able to differentiate between the types of discount. Ensure that you are aware of all of the discounts and how they differ.

Sales tax and settlement (cash) discounts

Sales tax and settlement (cash) discounts

The sales tax is calculated on the assumption that the settlement discount is taken, therefore on the net amount less the settlement discount.

When an invoice is issued it is not known whether the customer will take advantage of the settlement discount or not.

Example

Goods are despatched to a customer with a list price of £1,000. The customer is allowed a trade discount of 20% and is offered a settlement discount of 4% if the invoice is paid within 10 days.

Invoice amounts:

	£
List price	1,000.00
Less: trade discount	(200.00)
	800.00
Sales tax (see below)	153.60
Invoice total	953.60
Sales tax calculation (£800 x 96% x 20%)	153.60

NB The sales tax has been calculated based on £800 (list price less trade discount) less a settlement discount of 4% (therefore 96% of £800).

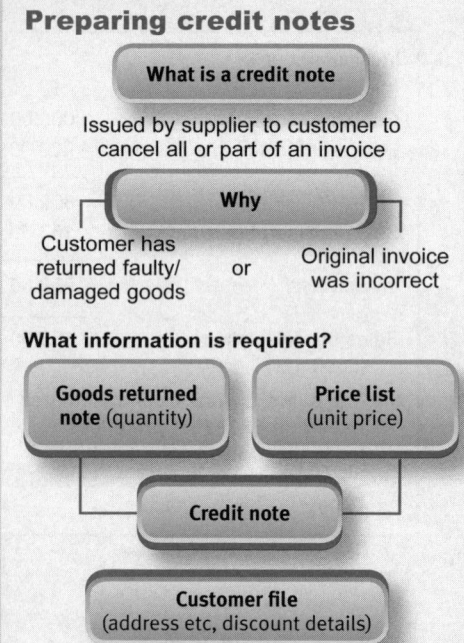

Preparing credit notes

What is a credit note

Issued by supplier to customer to cancel all or part of an invoice

Why

Customer has returned faulty/ damaged goods

or

Original invoice was incorrect

What information is required?

Goods returned note (quantity)

Price list (unit price)

Credit note

Customer file (address etc, discount details)

Coding

- relevant to most business documents not just sales invoices/credit notes
- quick, simple method of analysing information for further processing.

Coding and sales invoices/credit notes

- code required for product/type of sale
- customer account code for posting to sales ledger.

Coding systems

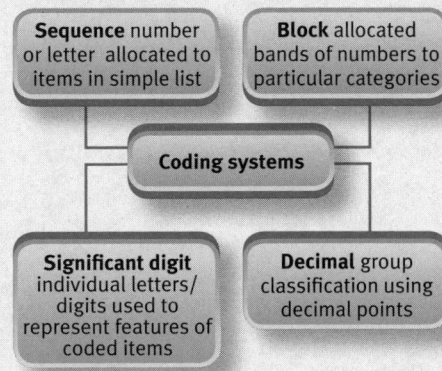

Sequence number or letter allocated to items in simple list

Block allocated bands of numbers to particular categories

Coding systems

Significant digit individual letters/ digits used to represent features of coded items

Decimal group classification using decimal points

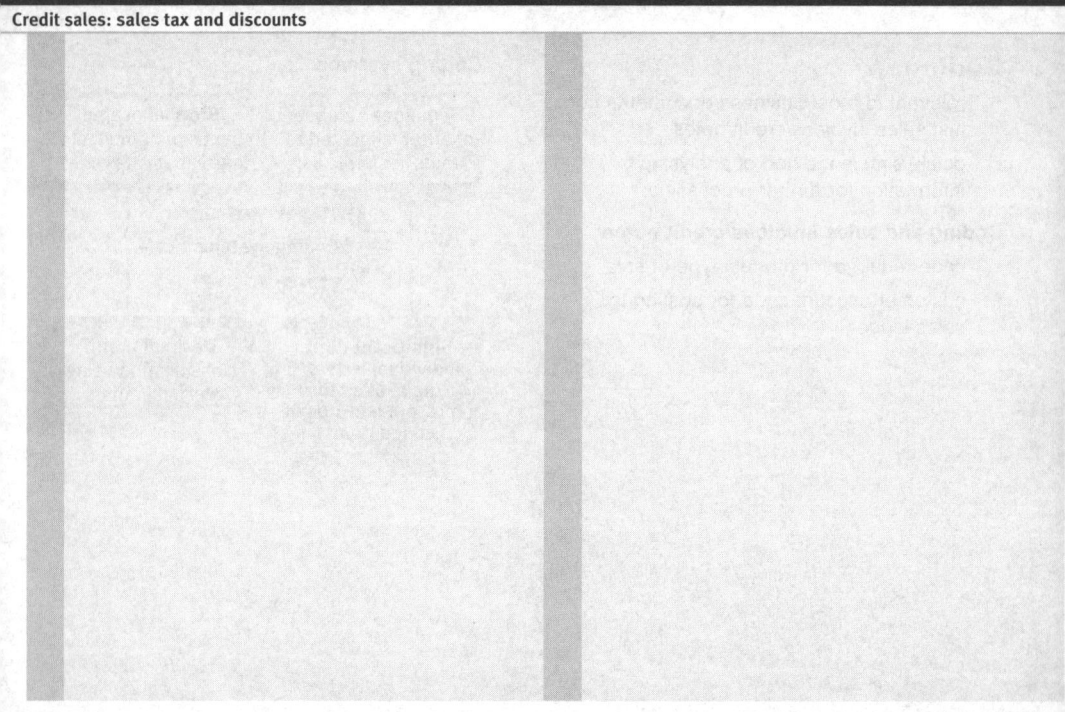

6

Sales day book – general and subsidiary ledgers

- Books of prime entry.
- Sales day book.
- Sales returns day book.
- Posting the sales day book.
- Posting the sales returns day book.

Books of prime entry

Rather than entering each individual transaction into the ledger accounts as they happen, books of prime entry are used to record transactions/documents of the same type before they are processed further.

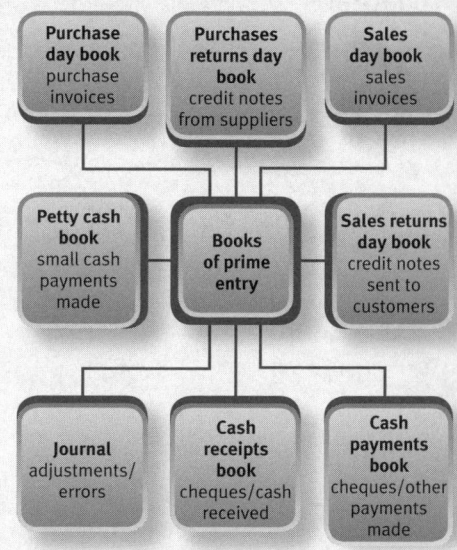

Sales day book

- list of invoices sent out to credit customers
- date
- invoice number
- customer name/account code
- invoice total analysed into net, sales tax and gross (total).

- information copied from sales invoices
- before further processing must be totalled
- totals can be checked by cross casting £3,794.14 + £758.82 = £4,552.96.

Sales Day book						
Date	Invoice No	Customer Name	Sales ledger code	Total (gross) £	Sales tax (20%) £	Net £
12/08/X3	69489	TJ Builder	SL21	2,004.12	334.02	1,670.10
12/08/X3	69490	McCarthy & Sons	SL08	1,485.74	247.62	1,238.12
12/08/X3	69491	Trevor Partner	SL10	1,063.10	177.18	885.92
				4,552.96	758.82	3,794.14

Analysed sales day book

Sometimes the net figure (actual sales) is analysed into different types of sale/product type.

Sales day book										
Date	Invoice No	Customer Name	Code	Total (gross) £	Sales tax £	Russia £	Poland £	Spain £	Germany £	France £
15/08/X1	167	Worldwide News	W5	3,000.00	500.00					2,500.00
	168	Local News	L1	240.00	40.00			200.00		
	169	The Press Today	P2	360.00	60.00				300.00	
	170	Home Call	H1	240.00	40.00			200.00		
	171	Tomorrow	T1	120.00	20.00					100.00
	172	Worldwide news	W5	3,600.00	600.00	3,000.00	–			
				7,560.00	1,260.00	3,000.00	–	400.00	300.00	2,600.00

Sales returns day book

- list of credit notes sent out to credit customers
- date
- credit note number
- customer name/account code
- credit note total analysed into net, sales tax and total
- information copied from credit note.

SALES RETURNS DAY BOOK						
Date	Credit Note No.	Customer Name	Code	Total (gross) £	Sales tax £	Net £
28/08/X3	03561	Trevor Partner	SL10	125.48	20.91	104.57
28/08/X3	03562	TJ Builder	SL21	151.74	25.29	126.45
				277.22	46.20	231.02

Posting the sales day book

General ledger

- at the end of each day/week/month SDB is totalled
- totals must then be posted to accounts in the general ledger.

Double entry:

Debit	Sales Ledger Control Account	Total (gross) figure
Credit	Sales account	Net figure
Credit	Sales tax account	Sales tax amount

SALES DAY BOOK

Date	Invoice No	Customer Name	Sales ledger code	Total (gross) £	Sales tax £	Net £
12/08/X3	69489	TJ Builder	SL21	2,004.12	334.02	1,670.10
12/08/X3	69490	McCarthy & Sons	SL08	1,485.74	247.62	1,238.12
12/08/X3	69491	Trevor Partner	SL10	1,063.10	177.18	885.92
				4,552.96	758.82	3,794.14

Debit sales ledger control account

Credit sales tax

Credit sales

Sales Ledger Control Account

	£		£
SDB	4,552.96		

Sales account

	£		£
		SDB	3,794.14

Sales tax

	£		£
		SDB	758.82

Subsidiary (sales) ledger

- SLCA records the amount owing by all of the business's credit customers in total
- but also need information about each individual credit customer's balance
- therefore ledger account kept for each individual customer in a subsidiary ledger, the subsidiary (sales) ledger.

Subsidiary (sales) ledger

Customer A

	£		£

Customer B

	£		£

Customer C

	£		£

Posting to the subsidiary (sales) ledger

- each individual entry from the sales day book must be entered into the relevant customer account in the subsidiary (sales) ledger
- amount entered is the gross invoice total (including sales tax)
- entered on the debit side of the account indicating that this is the amount the receivable owes.

Example

Now we return to the sales day book from earlier and post the individual entries to the subsidiary (sales) ledger.

TJ Builder			
	£		£
SDB	2,004.12		

McCarthy & Sons			
	£		£
SDB	1,485.74		

Trevor Partner			
	£		£
SDB	1,063.10		

Posting the sales returns day book

- as with the SDB the SRDB must also be posted to the general ledger accounts and subsidiary (sales) ledger accounts.

General ledger

Double entry:
Debit Sales returns account Net figure
Debit Sales tax account Sales tax total
Credit Sales Ledger
Control Account Total (gross) figure

Sales Ledger Control Account

	£		£
SDB	4,552.96	SRDB	277.22

Sales account

	£		£
		SDB	3,794.14

Sales tax account

	£		£
SRDB	46.20	SDB	758.82

Sales returns account

	£		£
SRDB	231.02		

Subsidiary (sales) ledger

Each individual credit note must be entered in the customer's account:

- gross credit note total
- credit individual receivable account (reducing the amount owed).

T J Builder

	£		£
SDB	2,004.12	SRDB	151.74

McCarthy & Sons

	£		£
SDB	1,485.74		

Trevor Partner

	£		£
SDB	1,063.10	SRDB	125.48

CBA focus

In the examination you will be required to post the sales day book/sales returns day book and the purchases day book/purchases returns day book to the general ledger and the relevant subsidiary ledger.

Checking receipts

- Cheques.
- Other methods of receiving payment.
- Receiving money for credit sales.
- Checking settlement discounts.
- Paying in slip.
- Bank statement.
- Clearing system.

Cheques

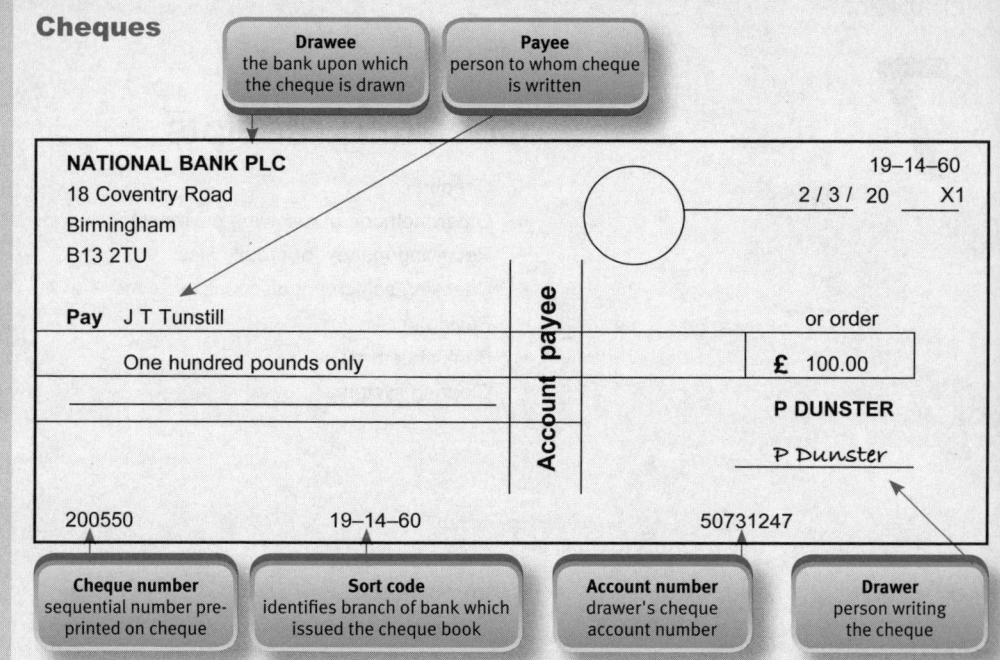

Drawee
the bank upon which the cheque is drawn

Payee
person to whom cheque is written

NATIONAL BANK PLC
18 Coventry Road
Birmingham
B13 2TU

19–14–60
2 / 3 / 20   X1

Pay J T Tunstill

Account payee

or order

One hundred pounds only

£ 100.00

P DUNSTER

P Dunster

200550

19–14–60

50731247

Cheque number
sequential number pre-printed on cheque

Sort code
identifies branch of bank which issued the cheque book

Account number
drawer's cheque account number

Drawer
person writing the cheque

Checks to make when receiving cheques

> **Date**
> cannot be postdated i.e. dated later than today's date
> - must be less than 6 months old – cheques are considered out of date after 6 months.

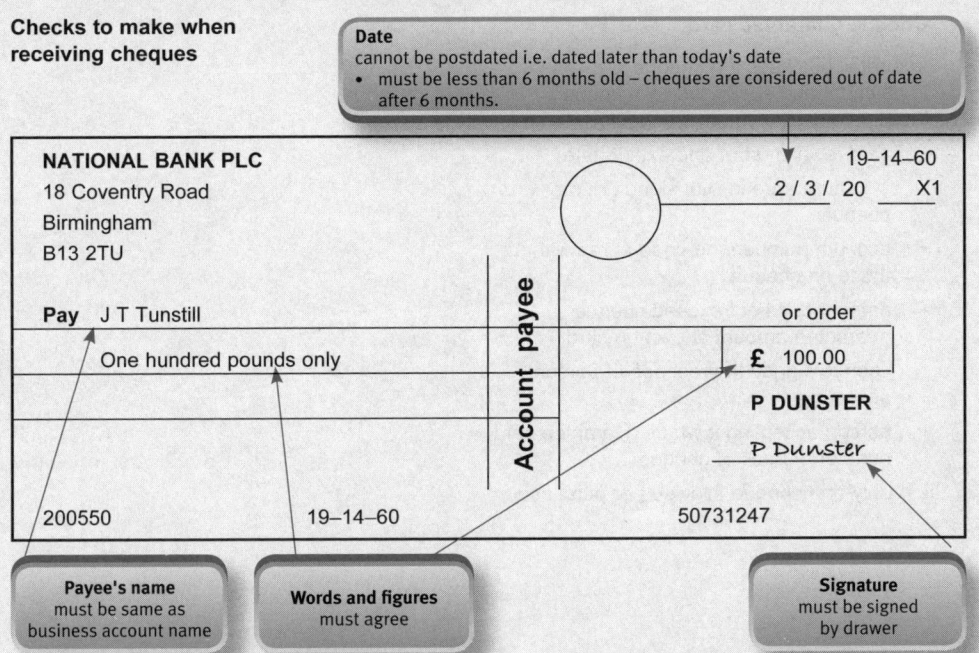

NATIONAL BANK PLC
18 Coventry Road
Birmingham
B13 2TU

19–14–60
2 / 3 / 20 ___ X1

Pay J T Tunstill   or order

One hundred pounds only   **£** 100.00

Account payee

P DUNSTER

P Dunster

200550   19–14–60   50731247

Payee's name
must be same as business account name

Words and figures
must agree

Signature
must be signed by drawer

Cheque guarantee card

In a retail business if a cheque is given in payment and supported by a cheque guarantee card – you must check:

- card is valid (start and expiry date)
- signature agrees with signature on cheque
- account number/sort code agree with those on cheque
- amount does not exceed cheque guarantee amount shown on card
- cheque signed in presence of person accepting it
- person accepting it writes guarantee card number of back of cheque
- only one cheque allowed per purchase.

Cheque crossings

What is a crossing? Two vertical lines across cheque – usually with words

The 'account payee' crossing is the normal crossing on a pre-printed cheque – it means the cheque can only be paid into the bank account of the payee.

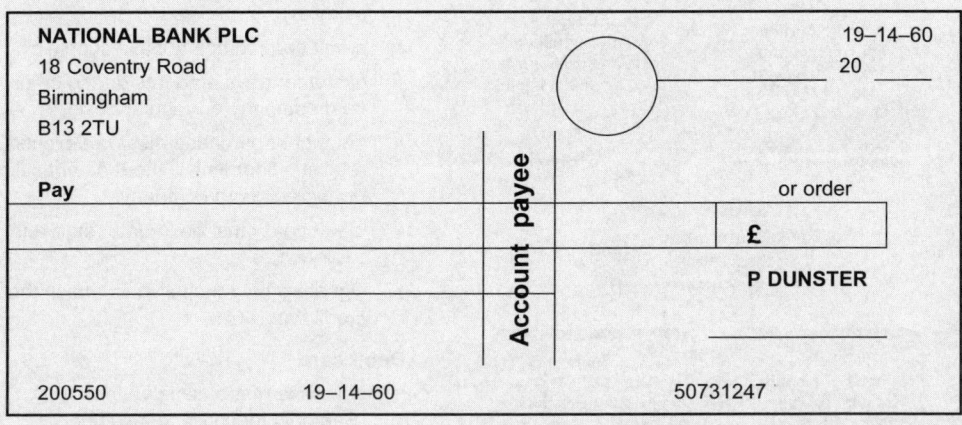

Other methods of receiving payment

Automated payments

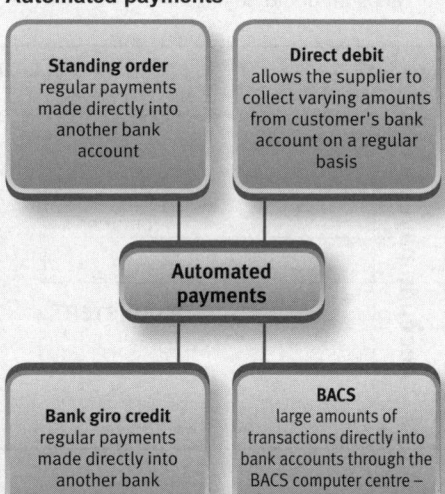

Standing order
regular payments made directly into another bank account

Direct debit
allows the supplier to collect varying amounts from customer's bank account on a regular basis

Automated payments

Bank giro credit
regular payments made directly into another bank account

BACS
large amounts of transactions directly into bank accounts through the BACS computer centre – often used for wages and salaries payments

Credit card and debit cards

Credit card

- purchases made using credit card voucher/PIN (Personal Identification Number)
- credit card company pays supplier
- customer pays amounts due to credit card company on regular basis
- amount of purchase must not exceed retailer's floor limit without authorisation from credit card company
- credit card must be in date (start and expiry date)
- signature on voucher must match that on credit card.

Debit card

- purchase made using voucher/PIN (Personal Identification Number)
- money transferred directly from customer's bank account to supplier's bank account.

Receiving money for credit sales

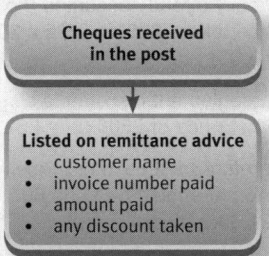

Cheques received in the post

↓

Listed on remittance advice
- customer name
- invoice number paid
- amount paid
- any discount taken

Remittance advice

- detachable slip on bottom of invoice/ statement

- returned by customer showing which invoices are being paid.

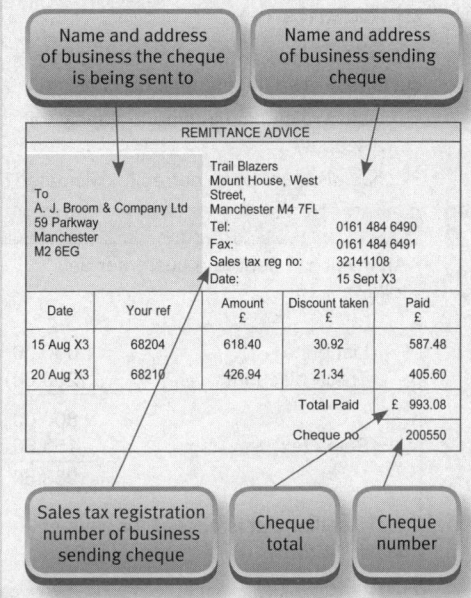

Name and address of business the cheque is being sent to

Name and address of business sending cheque

REMITTANCE ADVICE				

To
A. J. Broom & Company Ltd
59 Parkway
Manchester
M2 6EG

Trail Blazers
Mount House, West Street,
Manchester M4 7FL
Tel: 0161 484 6490
Fax: 0161 484 6491
Sales tax reg no: 32141108
Date: 15 Sept X3

Date	Your ref	Amount £	Discount taken £	Paid £
15 Aug X3	68204	618.40	30.92	587.48
20 Aug X3	68210	426.94	21.34	405.60
			Total Paid	£ 993.08
			Cheque no	200550

Sales tax registration number of business sending cheque

Cheque total

Cheque number

Checking settlement discounts

If a settlement discount is deducted by a customer – two things must be checked:

- was invoice paid in time to qualify for discount?
- has discount been correctly calculated?

Example

An invoice is sent to a customer as follows:

	£
List price	1,000.00
Trade discount	(200.00)
	800.00
Sales tax	153.60
	953.60

A 4% settlement is offered for payment within 14 days.

Note that the sales tax calculation has correctly already assumed the discount will be taken (£800 x 96% x 20% = £153.60).

The settlement discount is simply 4% of the net price of £800.00 = £32.00.

Therefore total payment received from the customer should be £953.60 – £32.00 = £921.60.

Recording the discount

- discount taken must be recorded either on the back of the cheque or the remittance list for further processing.

KAPLAN PUBLISHING

Paying in slip

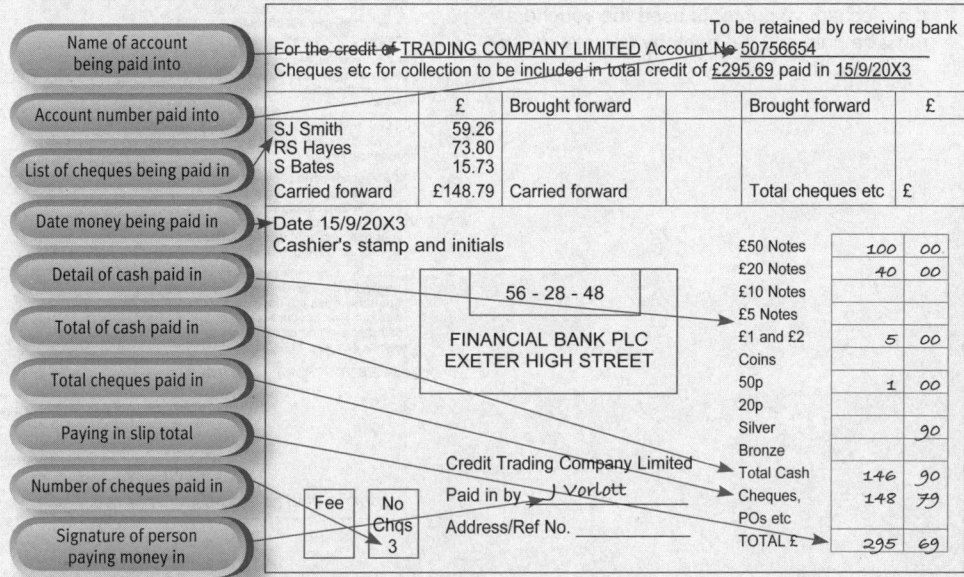

Name of account being paid into

Account number paid into

List of cheques being paid in

Date money being paid in

Detail of cash paid in

Total of cash paid in

Total cheques paid in

Paying in slip total

Number of cheques paid in

Signature of person paying money in

To be retained by receiving bank

For the credit of TRADING COMPANY LIMITED Account No 50756654
Cheques etc for collection to be included in total credit of £295.69 paid in 15/9/20X3

	£	Brought forward		Brought forward	£
SJ Smith	59.26				
RS Hayes	73.80				
S Bates	15.73				
Carried forward	£148.79	Carried forward		Total cheques etc	£

Date 15/9/20X3
Cashier's stamp and initials

56 - 28 - 48

FINANCIAL BANK PLC
EXETER HIGH STREET

Credit Trading Company Limited
Paid in by J Vorlott
Address/Ref No. _____

Fee	No Chqs 3

£50 Notes	100	00
£20 Notes	40	00
£10 Notes		
£5 Notes		
£1 and £2	5	00
Coins		
50p	1	00
20p		
Silver		90
Bronze		
Total Cash	146	90
Cheques, POs etc	148	79
TOTAL £	295	69

Credit card sales

If a mechanical printer is used the vouchers must be paid into the bank by completing the retail voucher summary:

Back of summary

Please do not pin or staple this voucher as this will affect the machine processing.

All sales vouchers must be deposited within three banking days of the dates shown on them.

If you are submitting more than 26 vouchers please enclose a separate listing.

If a voucher contravenes the terms of the retailer agreement then the amount shown on the voucher may be charged back to your bank account, either direct or via your paying in branch.

Similarly, if the total amount shown on the Retail Voucher Summary does not balance with our total of vouchers, the difference will be credited (or debited) to your bank account.

	£	p
1		
2		
3		
4		
5		
6		
7		
8		
9		
10		
11		
12		
13		
14		
15		
16		
17		
18		
19		
20		
21		
22		
23		
24		
25		
26		

SALES VOUCHERS   TOTAL

	£	p
1		
2		
3		
4		
5		
6		
7		

REFUND VOUCHERS   TOTAL

Front of Summary

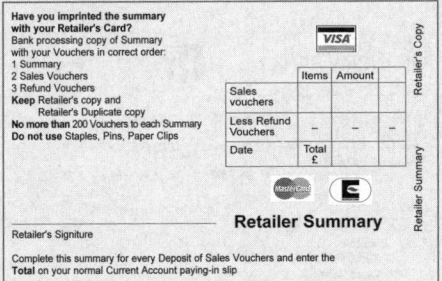

Have you imprinted the summary
with your Retailer's Card?
Bank processing copy of Summary
with your Vouchers in correct order:
1 Summary
2 Sales Vouchers
3 Refund Vouchers
Keep Retailer's copy and
        Retailer's Duplicate copy
No more than 200 Vouchers to each Summary
Do not use Staples, Pins, Paper Clips

VISA

Retailer's Copy

	Items	Amount
Sales vouchers		
Less Refund Vouchers	–	–	–
Date	Total £	

MasterCard

Retailer Summary

Retailer Summary

Retailer's Signiture

Complete this summary for every Deposit of Sales Vouchers and enter the
Total on your normal Current Account paying-in slip

Electronic credit card sales

Most credit card sales nowadays are
electronic using the PIN system therefore
there is no need to pay anything into the
bank.

Use of paying in slip

- before taking the cash/cheques/credit
  card vouchers/paying in slip to the bank
  it will normally be photocopied so that
  it can be used for entering the amounts
  paid in into the cash receipts book

- if the paying in slip is to be used to
  write up the cash receipts book then
  the amount of any settlement discount
  taken by any credit customers must be
  recorded together with the amount of the
  cheque received from them.

Bank statement

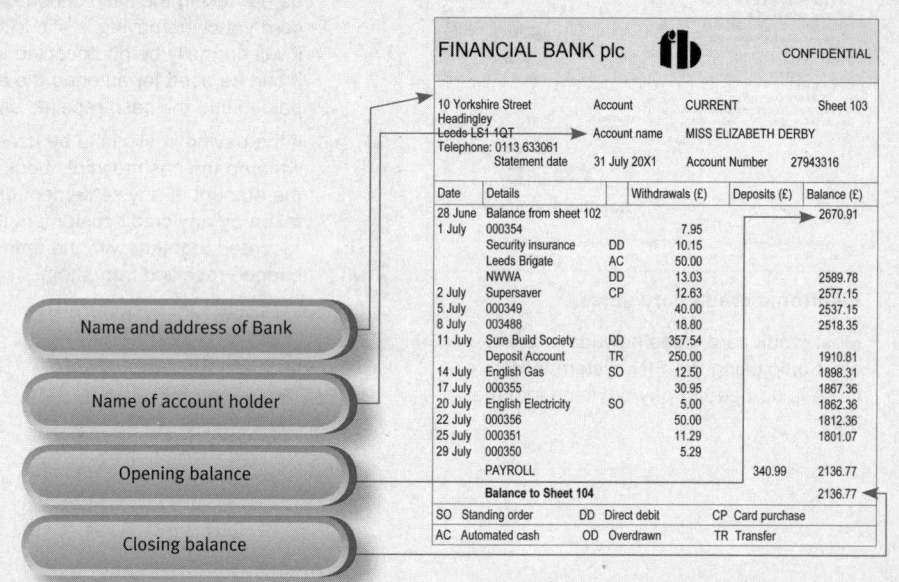

FINANCIAL BANK plc   **fb**   CONFIDENTIAL

10 Yorkshire Street   Account   CURRENT   Sheet 103
Headingley
Leeds LS1 1QT   Account name   MISS ELIZABETH DERBY
Telephone: 0113 633061
     Statement date   31 July 20X1   Account Number   27943316

Date	Details		Withdrawals (£)	Deposits (£)	Balance (£)
28 June	Balance from sheet 102				2670.91
1 July	000354		7.95		
	Security insurance	DD	10.15		
	Leeds Brigate	AC	50.00		
	NWWA	DD	13.03		2589.78
2 July	Supersaver	CP	12.63		2577.15
5 July	000349		40.00		2537.15
8 July	003488		18.80		2518.35
11 July	Sure Build Society	DD	357.54		
	Deposit Account	TR	250.00		1910.81
14 July	English Gas	SO	12.50		1898.31
17 July	000355		30.95		1867.36
20 July	English Electricity	SO	5.00		1862.36
22 July	000356		50.00		1812.36
25 July	000351		11.29		1801.07
29 July	000350		5.29		
	PAYROLL			340.99	2136.77
	Balance to Sheet 104				2136.77

SO	Standing order	DD	Direct debit	CP Card purchase
AC	Automated cash	OD	Overdrawn	TR Transfer

Name and address of Bank

Name of account holder

Opening balance

Closing balance

A statement tends to be received periodically from the bank detailing receipts to and payments from the account.

Terminology

When you have money in your bank account the bank says you are IN CREDIT.

When you have an overdraft the bank says you have a DEBIT BALANCE.

This terminology may seem to be opposite to that used in the ledger accounts but it is just that the bank statement is looking at the account balance in the bank's point of view.

Therefore a debit balance in the business's ledger account means there is cash in the account and this will be called a credit balance by the bank (because the bank owes this to the business) and vice versa.

Clearing system

All of the UK high street banks are involved in the clearing system which is a method by which the banks exchange cheques.

The relevance of the clearing system to a bank reconciliation is that when cheques is that when cheques are paid into the bank account it will take three working days before the money is credited to the business bank account.

CBA focus

When preparing bank reconciliation statements (as examined within Basic Accounting II) you will find outstanding lodgements and unpresented cheques which are largely due to the time delay caused by the clearing system.

Cash receipts book

- Cash receipts book.
- Sales tax.
- Settlement discounts.
- Posting the cash receipts book to the general ledger.
- Posting the cash receipts book to the subsidiary ledger.

Cash receipts book

The cash receipts book records all money received into the business bank account for whatever reason.

Cash receipts book							
Date	Narrative	Total £	Sales tax £	Receivables £	Cash sales £	Sundry £	Discount £
3 Jul	A Brown	20.54	3.42		17.12		
5 Jul	S Smith & Co Ltd	9.30		9.30			
	P Priest	60.80		60.80			
	James & Jeans	39.02	6.50		32.52		
	LS Moore	17.00		17.00			1.00
6 Jul	L White Ltd	5.16		5.16			
7 Jul	M N Furnishers Ltd	112.58				112.58	
	R B Roberts	23.65		23.65			2.29
	Light and Shade	86.95		86.95			
		375.00	9.92	202.86	49.64	112.58	3.29

| Date of receipt | Details of receipt | Total of receipts | Total Sales tax on cash sales | Total receipts from receivables | Total receipt for cash sales | Total receipts from sundry income | Total discounts allowed |

- entries to the cash receipts book come from either the remittance list or a photocopy of the paying in slip
- to check the totalling the cross casts should be checked:

	£
Sales tax	9.92
Receivables	202.86
Cash sales	49.64
Sundry income	112.58
Total	375.00

CBA focus

When you are cross-casting the cash receipts book make sure that you do not include the discounts allowed column as this is a completely separate memorandum entry and is not part of the total paid into the bank.

Sales tax

- Sales tax is only ever recorded in the cash receipts book on cash sales or other income

- any sales tax on sales on credit (i.e. receipts from receivables) has already been recorded in the sales day book and posted to the ledger accounts from there.

Settlement (cash) discounts

- settlement/cash discounts taken by customers are called discounts allowed

- they must be initially recorded either on the remittance list or paying-in slip

- then recorded in the discounts allowed column in the cash receipts book.

Posting the cash receipts book to the general ledger

Basic double entry for cash receipts :

Debit   Bank account
Credit   Sales Ledger Control Account
         (receipts from receivables)
         Sales (cash sales)
         Other income (e.g. rent)

In most cases the cash receipts book is not only a book of prime entry but also part of the general ledger in which case the debit entry for the total column is not required.

Postings

Cash receipts book							
Date	Narrative	Total £	Sales tax £	Receivables £	Cash sales £	Sundry £	Discount £
3 Jul	A Brown	20.54	3.42		17.12		
5 Jul	S Smith & Co Ltd	9.30		9.30			
	P Priest	60.80		60.80			
	James & Jeans	39.02	6.50		32.52		
	LS Moore	17.00		17.00			1.00
6 Jul	L White Ltd	5.16		5.16			
7 Jul	M N Furnishers Ltd	112.58				112.58	
	R B Roberts	23.65		23.65			2.29
	Light and Shade	86.95		86.95			
		375.00	9.92	202.86	49.64	112.58	3.29

Credit sales tax account

Credit sales ledger control account

Credit sales account

Credit sundry income account

Debit discounts allowed, Credit sales ledger control account

Discounts allowed

Posting of discounts allowed requires both sides of the double entry as this is a memorandum column.

Debit   Discounts allowed account
Credit   Sales Ledger Control Account

Discounts allowed account

	£		£
CRB	3.29		

Sales Ledger Control Account

	£		£
		CRB	3.29

Posting the cash receipts book to the subsidiary ledger

- after the totals have been posted to the general ledger from the cash receipts book the individual entries in the receivables column must be posted to the subsidiary (sales) ledger
- each cash receipt is credited to the individual receivable account (reduction of amount owing)
- each discount allowed is credited to the individual receivable account (reduction of amount owing).

Subsidiary sales ledger – postings (extracts)

Smith & Co Ltd

	£		£
		CRB	9.30

L S Moore

	£		£
		CRB	17.00
		CRB (discount)	1.00

9

Receivables' statements

- Receivables' statements.
- Aged debt analysis.

Receivables' statements

- sent by supplier to customer usually monthly
- reminder of amounts due.

INVOICE				
Invoice to Fitch & Partners 23 Emma Place Manchester M6 4TZ		NICK BROOKS 225 School Lane Weymouth, Dorset WE36 5NR Tel: 0149 29381 Fax: 0149 29382 Date: 30/04/X2		
Date	Transaction	Debit £	Credit £	Balance £
03/04	INV001	185.65		185.65
10/04	CN001		49.35	136.30
14/04	INV005	206.80		343.10
18/04	PAYMENT		136.30	206.80
21/04	INV007	253.80		460.60
26/04	INV008	192.70		653.30
May we remind you that our credit terms are 30 days With 3% discount for payment within 14 days				

Aged debt analysis

- internal document
- prepared for each individual customer
- shows the age of amounts outstanding
- useful for identifying slow paying/problem customers.

Customer	Total £	<30 days £	30 to 60 days £	>60 days £
H Hardy	689.46	368.46	321.00	–
L Framer	442.79	379.60	–	63.19
K Knight	317.68	–	169.46	148.22

10

Credit purchases documents

- Purchases on credit – documents.
- Ordering goods and services.
- Receiving goods.
- Credit notes.

Purchases on credit – documents

Documents issued during the making of purchases on credit:

Purchaser	Supplier

Purchase requisition
internal document filled out by department within purchasing business which requires the goods

Price enquiry
sent by purchaser to suppliers

Quotation
sent by supplier to purchaser detailing price/terms offered

Order confirmation
sent by supplier to purchaser confirming that transaction will go ahead

Purchase order
sent by purchaser to supplier agreeing to price/terms offered and confirming wish to proceed

Delivery note
sent by supplier to purchaser showing quantities/types of goods delivered

Sales invoice
sent by supplier to purchaser detailing amount/terms of payment due

Goods received note
internal document filled out by purchaser on receipt of goods detailing number/type of goods received

Credit note
sent by supplier to purchaser if goods are returned or original invoice incorrect

In the examination you will often be required to identify the various documents that are used within the sales and purchases cycle.

Ordering goods and services

Purchase order

Purchase requisition
- internal request to purchasing department for goods/ services
- authorised by department manager

Price enquiries
- purchasing department wants to find best price and terms from suppliers

Purchase quotations received
- purchasing department can now compare prices and terms and choose best supplier

Purchase order
- sent out to chosen supplier

Purchase order confirmation
- received from supplier confirming price, discounts delivery details

Purchase order

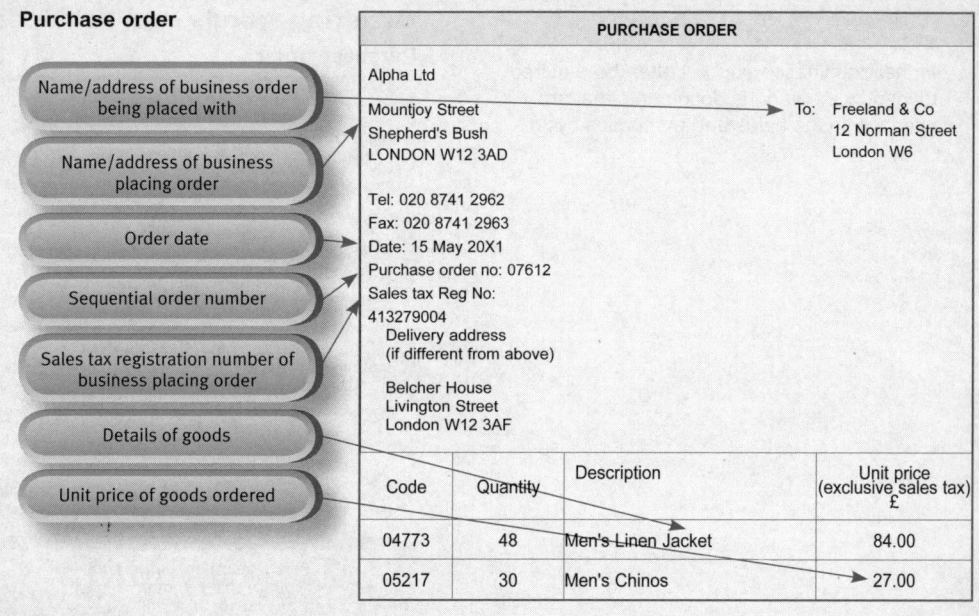

Name/address of business order being placed with

Name/address of business placing order

Order date

Sequential order number

Sales tax registration number of business placing order

Details of goods

Unit price of goods ordered

PURCHASE ORDER

Alpha Ltd

Mountjoy Street
Shepherd's Bush
LONDON W12 3AD

To: Freeland & Co
12 Norman Street
London W6

Tel: 020 8741 2962
Fax: 020 8741 2963
Date: 15 May 20X1
Purchase order no: 07612
Sales tax Reg No:
413279004
  Delivery address
  (if different from above)

  Belcher House
  Livington Street
  London W12 3AF

Code	Quantity	Description	Unit price (exclusive sales tax) £
04773	48	Men's Linen Jacket	84.00
05217	30	Men's Chinos	27.00

By telephone
if order placed by telephone details must be confirmed in writing

In writing

Ordering systems

By fax
- similar to in writing but quicker
- order confirmation required

Internet
- only used if allowed business policy
- copy of order must be printed and filed

Receiving goods

Delivery note

- accompanies goods from supplier
- details on delivery note must be checked to actual goods.

DELIVERY NOTE

Deliver to:
Fitch & Partners
Unit 15
Standford Business Park
Manchester
M13 8PB

A. J. Broom & Company Limited
Mountjoy Street
Shepherd's Bush
LONDON W12 3AD
Tel: 0161 560 3392
Fax: 0161 560 5322
Delivery note no: DN4A8372
Date: 25 August 20X3
Sales tax Reg No: 625 9911 58

Code	Description	Quantity
CJA991	Cashmere Jumper (adult) cream	50

Goods received in good condition   Print name P HARVEY

Signature P Harvey

Date 28/8/X3

- Delivery address
- Name/address of supplier
- Sequential delivery note number
- Date of delivery
- Sales tax registration number of supplier
- Details/quantity of goods
- Name and signature of person at purchaser's who checks and counts goods

Goods received note

- delivery note is checked as soon as goods arrive
- sometimes a further internal document is filled out once goods have been fully checked
- this is the goods received note
- this details number of goods received and also condition of goods – if some damaged this will be noted
- filed with delivery note.

Credit notes

Debit note and credit note

- if goods received are damaged or not what was ordered they will be returned to supplier
- purchaser may complete a debit note or returns note to accompany returned goods and explain reason for return
- credit note should be received from supplier.

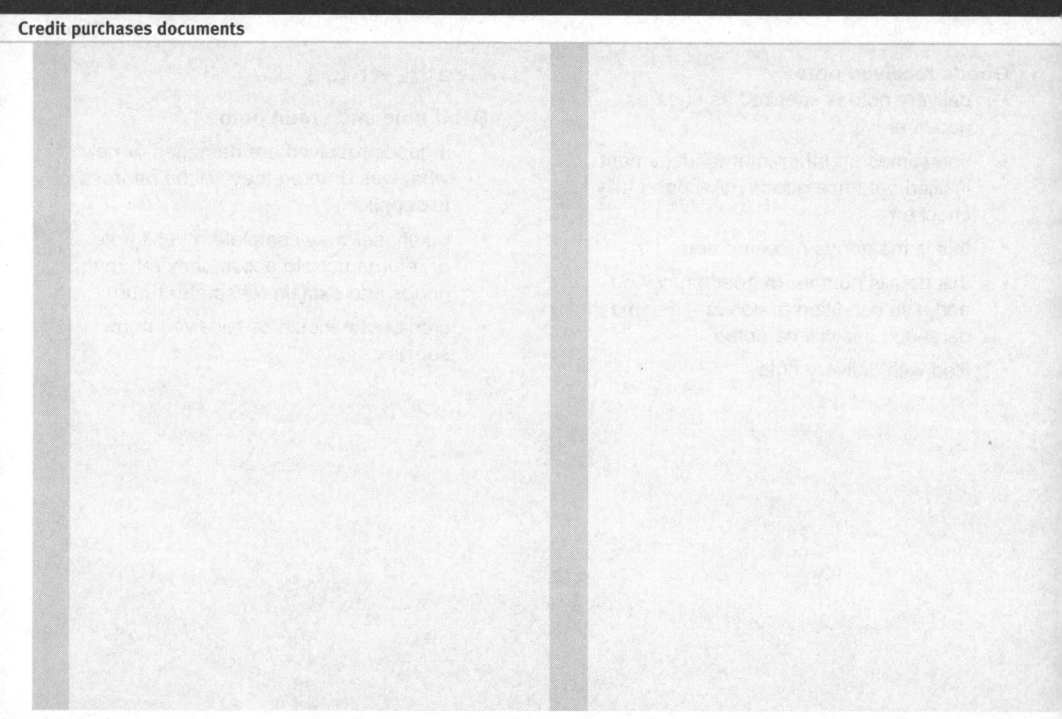

Credit purchases – discounts and sales tax

- Sales tax and settlement discounts.

Sales tax and settlement discounts

Sales tax and discounts have already been studied when considering sales in chapter 5. The calculations of Sales tax and discounts are exactly the same when considering purchases.

The purchaser receives a "sales invoice" from the seller but the purchaser refers to this as a "purchase invoice" and enters it into the books accordingly. It is the same document but is referred to differently by the different parties involved in the transaction.

Ensure that you are happy with the calculations of Sales tax and discounts by reviewing over these in chapter 5.

Purchases day book – general and subsidiary ledger

- Purchases day book.
- Purchases returns day book.
- Posting the purchases day book.
- Posting the purchases returns day book.

Purchases day book

- list of invoices received from credit suppliers
- date
- purchase invoice number (often internal consecutive number allocated)
- supplier name/account code

- invoice total analysed into net, Sales tax and total (gross)
- information copied from purchase invoice before further processing must be totalled
- totals can be checked by cross casting £663.90 + £132.77 = £796.67.

			PURCHASES DAY BOOK			
Date	Invoice No.	code	supplier	Total (gross) £	Sales tax £	Net £
20X1						
7 May	2814	PL06	J Taylor	190.41	31.73	158.68
8 May	2815	PL13	McMinn Partners	288.14	48.02	240.12
	2816	PL27	D B Bros	96.54	16.09	80.45
9 May	2817	PL03	J S Ltd	221.58	36.93	184.65
				796.67	132.77	663.90

Analysed purchase day book

Sometimes the net figure (actual purchases)
is analysed into different types of purchase/
product type.

			PURCHASES DAY BOOK						
Date	Invoice no	Code	Supplier	Total (gross) £	Sales tax £	01 £	02 £	03 £	04 £
05/02/X5	1161	053	Calderwood & Co	20.16	3.36	16.80			
05/02/X5	1162	259	Mellor & Cross	112.86	18.81		94.05		
05/02/X5	1163	360	Thompson Bros Ltd	42.86	7.14	35.72			

Purchases returns day book

- list of credit notes received from credit suppliers
- date
- credit note number (often internal consecutive number allocated)
- customer name/account code
- credit note total analysed into net, Sales tax and total
- information copied from credit note.

PURCHASES RETURNS DAY BOOK

Date	Credit note no	Supplier	Code	Total (gross) £	Sales tax £	Net £
09/05/X1	02456	McMinn Partners	PL13	64.80	10.80	54.00
09/05/X1	02457	J S Ltd	PL03	72.00	12.00	60.00
				136.80	22.80	114.00

Posting the purchases day book (PDB)

General ledger

- at the end of each day/week/month PDB is totalled
- totals must then be posted to accounts in the general ledger.

Double entry:

Debit	Purchases account	Net figure
Debit	Sales tax account	Sales tax amount
Credit	Purchases Ledger Control Account (PLCA)	Total (gross) figure

PURCHASES DAY BOOK

Date	Invoice No.	Code	Supplier	Total (gross) £	Sales tax £	Net £
20X1						
7 May	2814	PL06	J Taylor	190.41	31.73	158.68
8 May	2815	PL13	McMinn Partners	288.14	48.02	240.12
	2816	PL27	D B Bros	96.54	16.09	80.45
9 May	2817	PL03	J S Ltd	221.58	36.93	184.65
				796.67	132.77	663.90

Purchases account

	£		£
PDB	663.90		

Purchases ledger control account

	£		£
		PDB	796.67

Sales tax account

	£		£
PDB	132.77		

Subsidiary purchases ledger

- The PLCA records the amount owing to all of the business's credit suppliers in total
- but also need information about each individual credit supplier's balance
- therefore ledger account kept for each individual supplier in a subsidiary ledger, the subsidiary (purchases) ledger.

Subsidiary (Purchases) Ledger

Supplier A

£	£

Supplier B

£	£

Supplier C

£	£

Posting to the subsidiary (purchases) ledger

- each individual entry from the purchases day book must be entered into the relevant supplier account in the subsidiary (purchases) ledger
- amount entered is the gross invoice total (including Sales tax)
- entered on the credit side of the account indicating that this is the amount owed to the supplier.

Example continued

Now we return to the purchases day book from earlier and post the individual entries to the subsidiary (purchases) ledger.

J Taylor

£		£
	PDB	190.41

McMinn Partners

£		£
	PDB	288.14

D B Bros

£		£
	PDB	96.54

J S Ltd

£		£
	PDB	221.58

Posting the purchases returns day book (PRDB)

- as with the PDB the PRDB must also be posted to the general ledger accounts and subsidiary (purchases) ledger accounts.

General ledger

Double entry:

Debit	Purchases Ledger Control Account	Total (gross) figure
Credit	Purchases returns account	Net figure
Credit	Sales tax account	Sales tax total

Purchases account

	£		£
PDB	663.90		

Sales tax account

	£		£
PDB	132.77	PRDB	22.80

Purchase Ledger Control Account

	£		£
PDB	136.80	PDB	796.67

Purchases returns account

	£		£
		PRDB	114.00

Subsidiary (purchases) ledger

Each individual credit note must be entered in the supplier's account:

- gross credit note total
- debit individual supplier account (reducing the amount owing).

CBA focus

In the examination you will be required to post the sales day book/sales returns day and the purchases day book/purchases returns day book to the general ledger and the relevant subsidiary ledger.

J Taylor		
£		£
	PDB	190.41

McMinn Partners		
£		£
	PDB	288.14

D B Bros		
£		£
	PDB	96.54

J S Ltd		
£		£
	PDB	221.58

13

Making payments

- Checks to make on purchase invoices.
- Coding.
- Amount of payment.
- Scheduling of payments.
- Methods of payment.
- Cheque requisitions.
- Capital and revenue expenditure.

Checks to make on purchase invoices

Once a purchase invoice is received from a supplier a number of checks must be made on it to ensure that it is valid before it is authorised for payment.

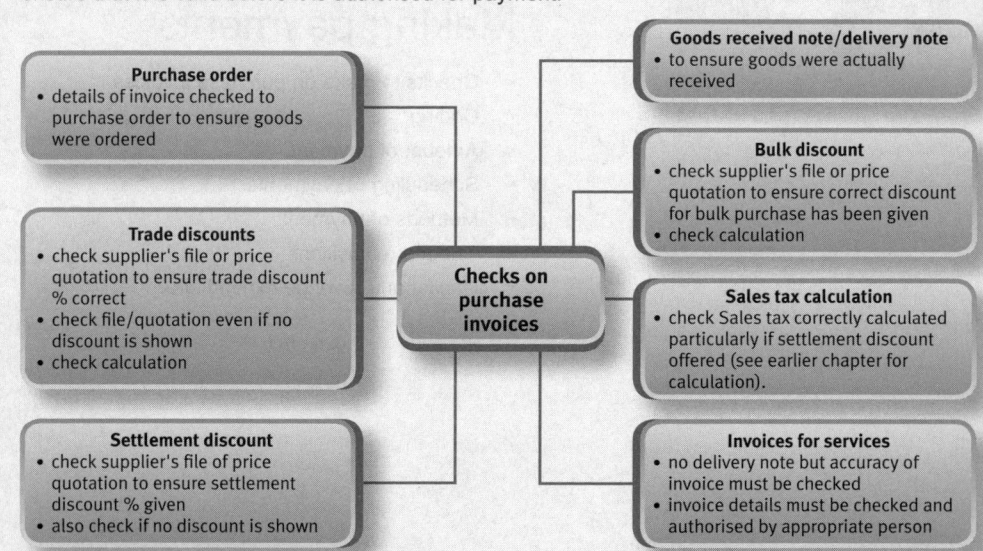

Purchase order
- details of invoice checked to purchase order to ensure goods were ordered

Trade discounts
- check supplier's file or price quotation to ensure trade discount % correct
- check file/quotation even if no discount is shown
- check calculation

Settlement discount
- check supplier's file of price quotation to ensure settlement discount % given
- also check if no discount is shown

Checks on purchase invoices

Goods received note/delivery note
- to ensure goods were actually received

Bulk discount
- check supplier's file or price quotation to ensure correct discount for bulk purchase has been given
- check calculation

Sales tax calculation
- check Sales tax correctly calculated particularly if settlement discount offered (see earlier chapter for calculation).

Invoices for services
- no delivery note but accuracy of invoice must be checked
- invoice details must be checked and authorised by appropriate person

Credit notes

The same checks as above should be made credit notes received from suppliers.

Coding

- purchase orders are coded with product type
- delivery notes are coded with product type
- purchase invoices will be coded with product type and supplier code
- credit notes will be coded with product type and supplier code
- often done by stamping purchase invoice/credit note with authorisation stamp.

Example of authorisation stamp

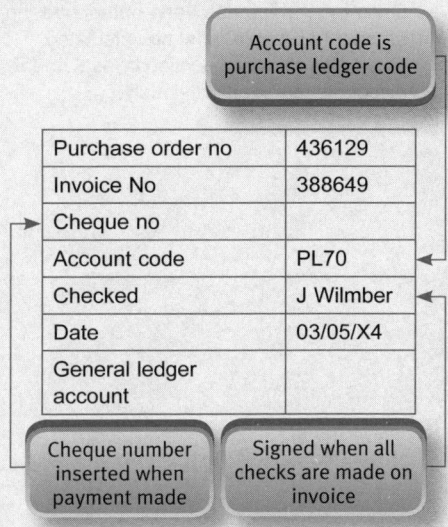

Account code is purchase ledger code

Purchase order no	436129
Invoice No	388649
Cheque no	
Account code	PL70
Checked	J Wilmber
Date	03/05/X4
General ledger account	

Cheque number inserted when payment made

Signed when all checks are made on invoice

Amount of payment

Once the invoice has been authorised the amount to be paid must be calculated. This may entail the complication of settlement discounts, as seen previously.

Example

An invoice is received from a supplier as follows:

	£
List price	1,000.00
Trade discount	(200.00)
	800.00
Sales tax	153.60
	934.40

A 4% settlement is offered for payment within 14 days.

Note that the Sales tax calculation has correctly already assumed the discount will be taken (£800 x 96% x 20% = £153.60).

The settlement discount is simply 4% of the net price of £800.00 = £32.00.

Therefore total payment to be made should be £953.60 – £32.00 = £921.60.

Scheduling of payments

Payment by invoice
- each invoice paid at latest date allowed by credit terms
- must ensure that if the business policy is to take cash discounts then invoice is paid in time to reach supplier within agreed period

Payment on set date
- this may be one day per week/month but this may mean that cash discounts are lost
- alternative to set day per week/fortnight when all invoices which will have exceeded credit/settlement discount limit by following payment date are paid

Methods of scheduling of payments

Payment of supplier's statements
- received monthly showing invoices outstanding
- must be checked to supplier's account to ensure correct
- invoices on statement will be paid according to business policy
- often remittance advice attached to statement to show amounts being paid

Methods of payment

These were considered in the earlier chapter on receiving payments. Instead of receiving payments from customers, the business is now making payments to suppliers.

Cheque requisitions

- required when there is no invoice or bill for a payment
- request for payment for such an expense
- must be authorised by senior person
- then cheque can be issued.

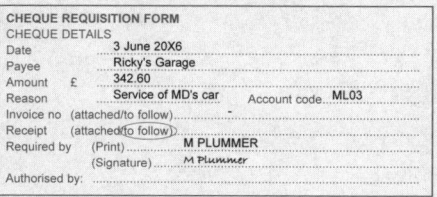

```
CHEQUE REQUISITION FORM
CHEQUE DETAILS
Date              3 June 20X6
Payee             Ricky's Garage
Amount      £     342.60
Reason            Service of MD's car    Account code.  ML03
Invoice no  (attached/to follow).................-
Receipt     (attached/to follow)).
Required by  (Print)............M PLUMMER
             (Signature)...........M Plummer
Authorised by:  .................................
```

Capital and revenue expenditure

You must be able to distinguish between the different natures of expense as it is a frequent skill required within the CBA.

CBA focus

Payments are made for all sorts of expenditure of different types. The important distinction is between capital expenditure and revenue expenditure.

Capital expenditure

- payment for the acquisition of non-current assets

- non-current assets are long term assets for use in the business rather than goods for resale or for other use in the business eg buildings, cars, machinery, computers, fixtures and fittings

- payment for the improvement of existing non-current assets eg replacing single glazed windows for double glazed windows.

Revenue expenditure

- all other types of expenditure which are not of a capital nature
- expenditure on day to day expenses eg rent, electricity, purchases of goods for resale, wages and salaries
- revenue expenditure is also any expenditure on repairs or maintenance of non-current assets. This means restoring a non-current asset to its original condition when first acquired by the business, not making any improvements to its original condition at acquisition.

14

Cash payments

- Cash payments book.
- Sales tax.
- Settlement discounts.
- Posting the cash payments book to the general ledger.
- Posting the cash payments book to the subsidiary ledger.

Cash payments book

The cash payments book records all money paid out of the business bank account for whatever reason.

Date	Details	Cheque No	Total	Sales tax	Purchase ledger £	Cash	Post	Discount
14/2	K Ellis	1152	80.00		80.00			2.00
15/2	Hutt Ltd	1153	120.00	20.00		100.00		
16/2	Biggs Ltd	1154	200.00				200.00	
			400.00	20.00	80.00	100.00	200.00	2.00

Date of payment — Details of payment — Total of payment — Total Sales tax on cash purchases — Total payment to payables — Total payment for cash purchases — Total payment for post — Total discounts allowed

- entries to the cash payments book come from either the cheque stubs or other banking documentation (see later chapter)
- to check the totalling the cross casts should be checked:

	£
Sales tax	20.00
Purchase ledger	80.00
Cash purchases	100.00
Post	200.00
Total	400.00

CBA focus

When you are cross-casting the cash payments book make sure that you do not include the discounts received column as this is a completely separate memorandum entry and is not part of the total paid out the bank account.

Sales tax

- Sales tax is only ever recorded in the cash payments book on cash purchases or other payments for expenditure that attracts Sales tax that have not been entered in the purchases day book.
- any Sales tax on purchases on credit (i.e. payments to payables) has already been recorded in the purchases day book and posted to the ledger accounts from there.

Settlement discounts

- settlement/cash discounts taken from suppliers are called discounts received
- they must be initially recorded on the cheque stub
- then recorded in the discounts received column in the cash payments book.

Posting the cash payments book to the general ledger

Basic double entry for cash payments :

Debit   Purchases for cash
Debit   Purchases ledger control account
Debit   Other expenses
Credit Bank account

In most cases the cash payments book is not only a book of prime entry but also part of the general ledger in which case the credit entry for the total column is not required.

Postings

Date	Details	Cheque No	Total	Sales tax £	Purchase ledger £	Cash purchases £	Post £	Discount received £
14/2	K Ellis	1152	80.00		80.00			2.00
15/2	Hutt Ltd	1153	120.00	20.00		100.00		
16/2	Biggs Ltd	1154	200.00				200.00	
			400.00	20.00	80.00	100.00	200.00	2.00

Debit Sales tax account

Debit purchases ledger control account

Debit cash purchases

Debit post

Debit purchases ledger control account, Credit discounts received

Discounts received

Posting of discounts received requires both sides of the double entry as this is a memorandum column.

Debit   Purchases ledger control account

Credit   Discounts received

Discounts received account

£		£
	CPB	2.00

Purchases Ledger Control Account

	£		£
CPB	2.00		

Posting the cash payments book to the subsidiary ledger

- after the totals have been posted to the general ledger from the cash payments book the individual entries in the purchase ledger column must be posted to the subsidiary (purchases) ledger
- each cash payment is debited to the individual payable account (reduction of amount owing)
- each discount received is debited to the individual payable account (reduction of amount owing).

Subsidiary (purchases) ledger – postings (extracts)

K Ellis

	£		£
CPB	80.00		
CPB (discount)	2.00		

CBA focus

In the examination you will be required
to post the cash book to both the general
ledger and the subsidiary ledger.

The cash book

- The cash book as part of the general ledger.

The cash book as part of the general ledger

The two sides of the cash book which are the cash receipts and the cash payments have been reviewed already as separate books.

The assessment often shows the cashbook as a ledger account format. This means that the cashbook actually forms a part of the general ledger, with the entries being one side of the double entry required within the general ledger.

The requirement will be to complete the other side of the entry within the general ledger, and to update the individual accounts in the subsidiary ledger.

16

Petty cash

- Petty cash system.
- Petty cash vouchers.
- Petty cash book.
- Posting the petty cash book.

Petty cash system

Most businesses require small amounts of cash for small cash expenses and reimbursement of business expenditure incurred by employees.

Petty cash box

- must be locked
- only petty cashier has access.

Employee incurs expense
eg. purchase stamps for office

↓

Fills out petty cash voucher for amount
and attaches receipt

↓

Takes to petty cashier who checks voucher
and receipt and authorises voucher

↓

Petty cashier gives employee amount spent out of
petty cash box and puts voucher in petty cash box

↓

Voucher is recorded in petty cash book

Petty cash vouchers

- gives details of expenditure incurred by employee
- must normally be supported by receipt or other evidence of expense
- must include Sales tax for expense where Sales tax is reclaimable
- must be authorised before payment can be made.

In the assessment you may be given a number of petty cash vouchers and be required to check them to ensure that they are valid.

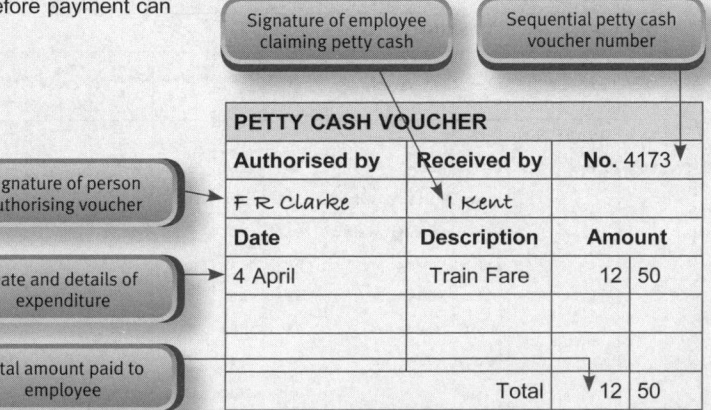

Signature of employee claiming petty cash

Sequential petty cash voucher number

Signature of person authorising voucher

Date and details of expenditure

Total amount paid to employee

PETTY CASH VOUCHER			
Authorised by	**Received by**	No. 4173	
F R Clarke	I Kent		
Date	**Description**	**Amount**	
4 April	Train Fare	12	50
	Total	12	50

Petty cash book

- book of prime entry
- often part of general ledger as well
- small cash receipts side
- larger analysed cash payments side.

Receipts side – only one column as only entry is regular payment in cash from bank

Payments side – analysed according to typical expenditure plus Sales tax column

Imprest amount of £150 to start week

Date of claim

Details

Sequestial petty cash voucher number

Analysed payments – total column includes Sales tax but analysis column amount is net of Sales tax

PETTY CASH BOOK

RECEIPTS			PAYMENTS								
Date	Narrative	Total £	Date	Narrative	Voucher no	Total £	Postage £	Cleaning £	Tea & Coffee £	Sundry £	Sales tax £
1 nov	Bal b/f	35.50									
1 nov	Cheque	114.50	1 Nov	ASDA	58	23.50			23.50		
			2 Nov	Post Office Ltd	59	29.50	29.50				
			2 Nov	Cleaning materials	60	15.07		12.56			2.51
			3 Nov	Postage	61	16.19	16.19				
			3 Nov	ASDA	62	10.57		8.81			1.76
			4 NOV	Newspapers	63	18.90				18.90	
			5 Nov	ASDA	64	12.10				10.09	2.01
						125.83	45.69	21.37	23.50	28.99	6.28

When petty cash book has been written up for a period it must be totalled. Totals should then be checked by cross-casting:

	£
Postage	45.69
Cleaning	21.37
Tea & coffee	23.50
Sundry	28.99
Sales tax	6.28
Total	125.83

Topping up the petty cash box

- at the end of the period (in this case a week) the petty cash box will be topped up to the imprest amount
- this is done by taking cash out of the bank account
- amount is total of the petty cash expenditure – £125.83
- petty cash box should then have imprest amount of £150 in order to start following week.

Posting the petty cash book (PCB)

Petty cash book part of general ledger

- petty cash book is normally part of the general ledger.

Receipt of cash

- debit entry already in petty cash book
- only posting required is a credit in the cash payments book for the cash taken out of the bank (this should have been done from cheque stub anyway).

Petty cash payments

- credit entry in petty cash book (total column £125.83)
- debit entries required to each expense account and Sales tax account.

Example

Postage account		
	£	£
PCB	45.69	

Cleaning account		
	£	£
PCB	21.37	

Food and drink acount		
	£	£
PCB	23.50	

Sundry expenses account		
	£	£
PCB	28.99	

Sales tax account		
	£	£
PCB	6.28	

Petty cash book not part of general ledger

- if the petty cash book is not part of the general ledger then a petty cash control account is required in the general ledger.

Petty cash receipt

- receipt of cash at start of week

  Debit Petty cash
      control account £114.50
  Credit Bank account   £114.50

Petty cash payments

Debit	Postage	£45.69
	Cleaning	£21.37
	Food and drink	£23.50
	Sundry expenses	£28.99
	Sales tax	£ 6.28
Credit	Petty cash control account	£125.83

CBA focus

The assessment may involve checking petty cash vouchers for validity, writing up and totalling the petty cash book and posting to the general ledger accounts.

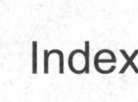

Index